BLURRED VISIONS AND WASTED NIGHTS

A.D. Winans

Contents

CITY POET

Once addiction sets in
There is no stopping it
You become a serial killer
Attack the keyboard at will

Your mind works in shifts
Strange creatures invade your head
Show no mercy give no ground
Force your fingers to do their bidding
Write down their thoughts
In your loose-leaf notebook

The City is your slaughterhouse
Like a spouse it accommodates your moods
Doesn't seem to mind you giving her a bad name

You walk her streets a hungry vampire
Lap up your own blood on nights when
Blood transfusions are not enough

.

GOING BACK IN TIME

I was looking at my scrapbook the other night while
listening to an old Dylan record
and there I was in my youth traveling from
California to Arizona and places further North
heading in so many directions
it was like being lost in the trick mirrors of the Fun House
at Play Land at the beach

and there were the young women then young girls
with free flowing spirits
who gave their minds and bodies
at the slightest invitation

and nights too laying alone in bed in tangled sleep
feeling like a deer caught in barbed wire
or sitting hunched-over cold and disheveled
at the downtown Greyhound Bus Station
fighting off the eyes of leering men
who preferred boys to women

now eighty-three and counting
I realize I was there and back so fast
like a train running out of track
returning home carrying my life in a knapsack
the days the months the years hung out to dry
like your mother's washing on a frail clothesline

GOING BACK IN TIME TWO

When I was young I drove to Salinas
And ran through the bean fields
Pretended I was James Dean in East of Eden

I stopped off in Monterey to walk Cannery Row
Imagined myself packing sardines in-between
Midnight conversations with Doc and the boys

I drove to Carmel and scribbled a poem on a cocktail napkin
That later became the Title for my first book of poems
But the rents were high and the job pay low
So in 1964 I took my first full time job in Modesto

Drove on weekends to Stockton's public square park
To share a toke with wino's
In Crow's Landing I drank with unemployed Mexicans
At run-down dives

In North Beach and the Mission District
I hung out with deadbeats and losers
Street people fighting junkie tremors
And cirrhosis of the liver

In the Fillmore I cut my teeth on jazz
Let Billie Holiday patch up my bleeding heart
In the Portrero I saw the last of the factory workers
Grow thinner like their paychecks

In the Tenderloin I drank with whores and prostitutes
Who opened their pocketbooks as freely as their legs

On Market Street I witnessed panhandlers crouched
Like criminals in open doorways
A short distance from the Jesus freaks
With God's billboards pointing the way to heaven

At the old Southern Pacific Railway Yard
I saw the last brakeman smoking a cigarette
With eyes vacant as an empty satchel

 On the other side of town high on Nob Hill
Society ladies sat In chauffeured limousines
White poodle dogs nestled between their piano legs
Unaware of the dredges of humanity
Walking third and Howard Street
Drinking cheap port from brown paper bags
Starving cold disheveled as the homeless are today
Waiting on god or pneumonia to walk them to the grave

COCAINE ANNIE

cocaine Annie biker queen
makes love to the jukebox machine
hands caress well shaped hips
eyes cowboy at the bar
digs her boots into the floor
wonders if he is worth a ride

tugs at black leather jacket
slides hands down jean-clad legs
heads out the door
opts for her Harley
guns the engine
heads down Highway 101
all the man she needs
vibrating between her well-shaped legs

CHINATOWN SWEAT SHOP

you see them coming but never going
working 12-14 hour shifts
6-7 days a week

I imagine the sewing machines humming
"A stitch in time saves nine."

you see them coming but never going.

I imagine the madam's eyes
an executioner in disguise
watching waiting as the Universe
grinds them into oblivion

SOUTH OF MARKET

you can see from the look in his eyes
the scar on his face
he's someone you don't want
to mess with

his eyes survey the scene like a periscope
he's a two-bit thug looking for action
an old beat cop looking for a head to bash
he's Boston Blackie and Al Capone
all rolled into one

his women are mean and lean
bred on the S & M scene
with tattooed flesh and black mesh
they walk the seedy side of town
looking to do the last waltz with you

in a back alley at South of Market
or in a basement dungeon
it's all the same all part of the game
doing a tap dance on your spine
looking dead serious like a sumo wrestler
sizing you up for the kill

OLD JOE

he sleeps in doorways or on park benches
or under the freeway
doesn't want to go to a shelter
not even when prodded with the weight
of the beat cop's nightstick

under threat of jail
he curls up in a fetal position
closes his eyes tries to shut out
the memories of Vietnam

nightmares whirl inside his head like
helicopter blades.

the alcohol the drugs the failed years
gather like locusts inside his brain
play all night rhapsodies inside his head

troubadour of Pharaoh origins
pale spokesman of lost tribes
masked as a homeless transient

poet prophet of beauty and imperfection
ravished by the streets kissed by angels
left tired withered like an unattended
Kansas grain field

SAINT ANTHONY BLUES

old men and women sit around
the community Rescue Mission dining table
eyes vacant as a demolished parking lot
nattily attired or in hand me down clothes

they sit somber like
wipe up the gravy from their plastic plates
with day old bread
a death sentence for eyes
folded handkerchiefs tucked away inside
the worn pocket of their souls

THE OLD PEOPLE OF DALY CITY

live in houses strung together
like tennis strings
windows filled with live corpses
with eyes that scan the streets like
a submarine periscope

inside the children glued to video games
as the rain hits the outside pavement
in machine-gun like bursts
scatter the adults like bowling pins

lady death arrives like the sound
of a jazz band
at a New Orleans street funeral

REALITY

the sound of the garbage truck
wakes me from my sleep
outside invisible vampires wait
for the nine-to-five crowd
when dreams turn to ham and eggs

CITY HAPPENINGS

they're having a rumble
at Ellis and Eddy streets
and the police are slow to respond

you can see the rage in the Latino's eyes
smell the fear in Whitey
the blacks shuck and jive
roll dice place bets
on winner and losers alike

the street whores move down a block
to ply their trade
one white one Asian one black

the cops arrive in mass
disperse the players like bit actors
auditioning for a bit role in the big show

small time punks gather themselves
run for cover
don't stop to look back

head for the crack house
bide their time like
a stoned Jesus hung out to dry
on a tattered clothesline

GIRLS OF THE TENDERLOIN

the girls of the tenderloin wear tank-tops
and short tight skirts
with white shoes that show off black skin
or black shoes that contrast white skin

the girls of the tenderloin
strut their stuff into the early dawn
stand out like a dragon
in a Chinese New Year Parade

move their hips suggestively
talk heavy thick slang
their "Hey Baby" you want a date"
cuts through the air like a machete
looking for a snake in knee-high grass

the girls of the tenderloin
walk talk strut their stuff
not afraid of the law man's bluff

the girls of the tenderloin
stop traffic with their looks
their dark brown eyes thirsty
as a Mexican Matador looking for a kill

WALKING THE MISSION
ON A HOT SUMMER DAY

he's standing on the corner
of sixteenth and Mission

looks tough in a tee shirt
and leather jacket
eighteen going on thirty

he's paring his fingernails
with a pocket knife
a tattoo of a snake
on the palm of one hand

he looks mean
he looks like he can take care of business
be it his or yours

men pass by avoid the look in his eyes
he works their fears like
a disc jockey in a groove
he wants to be the main man
the main attraction
here in the Mission
on a hot summer afternoon

DINING IN THE TENDERLOIN

I have sat one to many evenings
watching old men and women
eat their last meal
one eye on the dessert
the other on the obituary column

LIFE ON THE STREETS

It's an all night horror show
Hookers pimps transvestites
Transsexuals on the go

It's a night at the Top of the Mark
It's bathhouses and porno flicks
It's lonely vagina's in search of dicks

It's keystone cops and neon lights
It's drag queens in tights
It's the Phantom of the Opera
In a grotesque mask
It's a wino blood donor
It's a young man with a raging boner

It's CNN and the nightly news
It's John Lee Hooker singing the blues
It's apace aliens hiding out in Roswell
It's poor folks going through hell
It's pilgrims on the way to the Shrine
It's police informers dropping a dime
It's politicians wallowing in slime
It's a miracle it's a crime

It's a million windshield wipers
It's a billion disposable diapers
It' a 24-hours horror show
It's Larry Curly and Mo

It's doctors practicing the hypocritical oath
It's eating pussy and sucking cock
It's Al Capone doing time on The Rock

It's a waiter in a tux and bow tie
It's all one big lie
It's the way thing are
It's the nature of the beast
it's a famine it's a feast

it's babies crying
it's the elderly dying
It's the death of the Beats
It's life on the streets

POEM FOR A HOMELESS MAN

he stands in the rain
searches garbage cans
for pieces of treasure
an edible half-finished sandwich
a piece of bread
aluminum recycle cans
that he packs into his shopping cart
his home on wheels
limps off into the night talking
to the cracks in the street

WALKING THE STREETS AGAIN

I'm out walking the streets again
like a priest looking for a miracle
past Saint Paul's church where
the smell of altar boys permeates the air
the ripped-up street still hot from
the smell of freshly laid down tar

the tongues of harlots call out like
hungry birds diving for scraps of food
pass over the head of the aging Priest
who waves his hand in the air
as if in a private conversation with God
extends his hand to a wrinkled Italian woman
talking into her rosary beads
dusting off another miracle like
an aging cowboy back from
a long trail drive

WINTER POEM

Chill of winter in the air
Misty fog gives way to a light rain
Cars spew deadly exhaust fumes
Windshield wipers flap like
The wings of birds in migration

Stone faces hide behind steering wheels
Give no quarter yield only to the traffic lights
As pedestrians looking like mannequins
Turn into penguins scurry across the street
On their way to work
Board the morning commuter bus
Pressed together like preserved butterflies
Between the pages of an antique book

DOWN AND OUT

when I was young and down and out
and wrote from pain and anger
from my small apartment
on the fringe area of high crime
I was told by people of affluence
who enjoyed the company of poets
that it was good for me to be hungry
that this is what great writers are made of
and that someday I'd look back
on these days with fondness

now at 60
I've moved up to a one-room apartment
in a better part of town
with photographs of Josephine Baker
Billie Holiday Martin Luther King
and the Kennedy brothers on my walls
 to remind me of my commitment to civil rights

I've managed to put some money away
and my closets and icebox are nearly full
and I still have the same typewriter
that in the sixties and seventies
had me knocking at the door of success
a door that never fully opened

but whenever I think back on those days
it's not with fondness though I can't deny
that the women and parties weren't fun

and the typewriter rolled off poems
in great number
but the friends of affluence soon
parted company too

the truth is that the apartment
the lack of money and the roaches and mice
were more a matter of circumstances than necessity

you can go forward or you
can go back but the smell of shit
is still the smell of shit

they say that art creates itself
but I don't think I'll ever look back
 on those days with fondness

SAN FRANCISCO SKYLINE

San Francisco skyline blanketed in fog
Wears her history like a harlot
 In a tight fitting dress

Air sweet as a mango caresses her skin
She's a ballerina walking a high wire
Ghosts of her past dissolve into each other
Rooms of walls dare you to enter

Fists clenched like a boxer
She plays your mind like a card shark
Doors of Nirvana open and close
Like trick mirrors in a fun house

She's like an aging jockey
Looking for one more ride
On a magnificent horse
That crosses the finish line
Barely breaking a sweat

PIGEON FEATHERS

Holy men on every street corner
Selling fake myths
Nuns with virgin limbs
And mushroom dreams inside their loins

I am being followed by
Dick Tracy look-a-likes
With flat feet and bug eyes

The wolf's eerie howl
Haunts my dreams
Evangelists pickpocket
My empty wallet

My one good eye
Photographs the crime scene
The police lineup consists
Of six pygmies and a ham sandwich

Ladybugs ride on the wings of butterflies
On their way trip to Grace Land

God wanders the universe
Carries Jesus piggyback
On his way to a Madonna concert

The Holy Ghost confiscates my dreams
Holds me for a ransom I can't pay

The insatiable night eats my thoughts
I've become a one-legged tightrope walker
Without a safety net

My poems turn into pigeon feathers
Fly off with the wind

Old Warrior Of North Beach

(For Bob Kaufman)

He walks the streets of North Beach
Looking like an old man
With eyes empty as a broken parking meter

Unemployable weighed down by the years
His mind heavy as an anchor
Dragging the ocean floor

Forgotten rebel playing old Lorca ballads
In the shipwreck of his heart
His mind destroyed by shock treatments
And one too many police batons

At night he dreams he is riding with Geronimo
Has imaginary conversations with Charlie Parker
Rides the ferry with Coltrane and Mingus
Gets off at Bourbon Street to down
A drink with Kerouac

He shares a cigarette with Charlie Chaplin
At the old Bijou Theater
Walks the battlefields with Walt Whitman
Rides the plains with Red Cloud
In search of the last buffalo

Walks the streets of North Beach
In search of the elusive ginger fish smell
Death a sightless chauffeur waits like
A concubine facing another apocalyptic day

GOLDEN YEARS

it's been in the thirties
two nights in a row
and my heater went out
and I'm sitting here freezing
my ass off waiting for
the power company to come
and fix the problem

but it isn't so bad when
you consider Hurricane Katrina
earthquakes and tidal waves
and terrorism that plagues the world

thirty degree nights won't kill you
but they don't bring comfort either

the trouble with being single
the trouble with the golden years
is knowing you could die alone
and go undiscovered for weeks
with nothing but rotting flesh
to tell your story and a few poems
to remember you by

SUNDAY MORNING BLUES

there is this kind of motionless motion
children crying themselves to sleep
the taste of sunsets for breakfast
and champagne for lunch

there is this kind of mellow music
hills made of wild strawberries
salt on hard boiled eggs
Peanuts in the comic strips
and radio DJ's with god awful jokes
that see you through another morning

there is this kind of sadness
the feeling of a dull razor blade
sliding across smooth skin
Marilyn Monroe suicides and weekends
with nothing to do
heart attacks from love or lack of it
funerals with no mourners
poets with little future
and lovers with no one to love

POEM FOR THE JAZZ MAN AT THE BOTH AND CLUB

they say he's burned out
but no one has bothered to tell him
his Sax ignites a spark across the room
his lips work pure magic
each note attacking the
heart strings of the soul
and for one brief moment
he loses sight of the bubbling spoon
the heated needle
each note a burst of machine gun fire
just like he used to do before
the angel of death took him on
a straight line to hell

OPEN YOUR EYES

You can't escape it
Your remote control is wed to it
Local and cable channels feed it to you
Like meat thrown into a tigers cage

News of wars and pending wars
Reel you in like a doomed fish

You become part of it whether
You want to or not

You don't have to be on the front lines
To feel the wounds see the blood
Taste the carnage

Your parents and grandparents lived it
Willed it to you
As their parents before them

The dog feels it each time
He wags his tail

The cat hides under the bed
But can't escape it

Walt Whitman walked the battlefields
Bandaged the wounds of the fallen
William Carlos Williams saw it in
The faces of dying patients

General Grant tried to drink
The pain away

The disease can't be defeated
The Pope is powerless
The President embraces it
The First Lady dances with it
The vampire Congress feeds off it

It's a cancer that eats away at you
Sucks you down like quicksand

Admirals and Generals run through
The fields harvesting the dead
Politicians rattle their blood stained swords
In the midnight oil of democracy

Ballistic missiles pointed at the stars
The firing squad put on alert
Petrified standing like mannequins in a death field
The businessman's money tree
Bends with the weight
A nation in slave chains
Disguised as freedom

Turn on the TV open your eyes
It's all there to see

CHILDHOOD MEMORIES

It came into our lives unexpectedly
Like an unplanned child
Rudely shoved into the living room
Through the narrow doors
By two beer-bellied brutes
Grunting like pigs in heat

I remember it arriving
One hot summer afternoon
Charged on Dad's meager pay

Once in the house
Our lives were never the same

Many a night I would sneak from my bedroom
To peek through the door where
Mother and the beast engaged in battle
Like knights of old jousting for honor

Her eyes dream like
Each magical musical note
Bringing her back to kinder times
Before the weight of marriage crushed her
Like a bulldozer

Her fingers tickling the ivory keys
With tender notes of love
Looking like a Chinese sewing lady
In a garment shop as if each note was
A perfect stitch in time
Binding her life to a new scrap of cloth

WALKING THE BLUES AWAY

On my way home
I pass the park where
I used to play ball

The field is dry
The grass uncut
The diamond deserted

Just a group of teenagers
Loitering near the grandstand
Headphones stuck in their ears

I make my way to Martha's Cafe
For a cup of hot chocolate
To ward off the cold

A half-hour before nightfall
Feeling more alone than
At any time in my life

Soon I'll head home
Flip a TV dinner in the microwave
Turn on cable TV
Watch the evening news before
I slip into the bedroom
Slide between the sheets
Put on some jazz
Miles Davis or Charlie Parker
Try to fill the empty space
With notes that serenade the dead

UNTITLED

This empty room whispers dead secrets
Old ghosts appear disappear
Reappear to shake my hand

The telephone is the only one with connections
Says my agent who returns my manuscripts
Postage due

And you naked in the kitchen
Butcher knife in one hand looking
The part of a mad doctor hacking
The limbs off a dead tree

In the corner on the mantle
My father's old photograph
Looks down at me with accusing eyes

Death lurks everywhere
Licks every crevice of the room
She will find what she seeks
My grandmother warned me of this

Death the noble savage
Death the avenging sadist
Leaves behind her scars
Plays out the game to the bitter end
A giant hearse among a sea of compact cars

THOUGHTS ON THE CALIFORNIA DROUGHT

I sit here feeling like a used car
one part after the other failing me
early morning bacon sizzling on the grill

the drought laughs at the masses
teases them with a light drizzle

picture of an old lover stares down
at me from the mantle
her smile warm as the campfire
I sat around as a child

my room a dust garden
my hamstring pull refuses to address
the promised golden years drown in tears

Israel and Palestine engaged
in a never ending war

Putin plays death games in Moscow
proof the cave man still lives inside us

railroads and monuments built by immigrants
now treated like criminals

the elderly a liability
the young puppets in a political game

poets once warriors on skateboards
now prisoners of pride and envy

I take refuge in the soft raindrops
the peace of solitude rides my veins
like a steamship treading calm waters

the garden of my mind is still green
poems wait to be planted in fertile soil
no drought can kill

DINING OUT WHEN I WAS YOUNG

I didn't like it when my father
took me with him for lunch
at Foster's Cafeteria on Market Street

it wasn't the food that was OK
but the old folks I feared

the cook was fat and bald
and there was no waitress
and the bus boy was old
not a boy at all

the people who came there to eat
were retired people on low incomes
with death warrants for eyes
dabbing at their turkey-chins
with crumpled paper napkins
looking like pallbearers
back from a funeral

TOOL BOX POEM

last night while I was fighting insomnia
the demons created a toolbox inside my head
it is filled with every moment of my life
from the womb to the pending tomb

dead poets creep out at night
old flames appear disappear reappear
at the best years of their life

the toolbox has no lock
to keep unwanted visitors out

ghosts mock my past deeds
cavort with gypsy bands who travel
up and down my spine

Miles Davis plays his wailing magic
inside the symphony of my head

Muslim's wail Koran prayers
the Vatican closes its doors

a hurricane forms inside my brain
the fat lady at the opera does acrobats
from a high-tension wire

my woman says I'm damaged goods
leaves the door open on her way out

a used car salesman carries a frayed copy
of Death of a Salesman
in the palm of his sweaty hands

I dial the Jehovah Witness hot-line
it is busy 24/7
I call 9 1 1
I am put on hold

my poems turn into cue balls
explode on a green felt pool table
at Gino and Carlo Bar

my woman thinks she's Buddha
keeps her legs crossed

a witch doctors appears beside my bed
with a necklace of human bones
the voodoo doll in her hands
looks a lot like me

a gypsy woman shuffles a deck of tarot cards
God calls in his marker
turns me into an aging Samurai
with a dull bladed sword to fend off my enemies

the poems turn outlaw
hold me for a ransom I can't pay

the insatiable night eats my thoughts
the years rattle inside my head
like a bag of marbles

I toss and turn pray for sleep
but God has no time for insomniacs
the few hours granted me lined-up
like shots of tequila at a Mexican brothel

when sleep finally comes
I am left feeling like bits and pieces of a shipwreck
washed up along the shore of an island that doesn't exist
the toolbox empty as a tramp's turned out pockets

EATING CHINESE

I like eating Chinese
the tiny hot red peppers
hid in a spicy sauce

I like lean pork dipped
in hot mustard

I like curried chicken over
a bowl of steaming rice

I like tea and fortune cookies
I like the feel of chopsticks on my lips

I like Chinese waitresses
in white blouses and bow ties
I like eating Chinese

FOURTH OF JULY POEM

Stepped on pissed on cheated and abused
Taken advantage of blue collar man
Caught up in the American scam

Don't tell me anyone can be anything
They want to be
If they put their mind to it

Save your BS for the deaf dumb and blind
It'll never sell in the ghetto
Or to the immigrants
You've turned your back on

Take your message to the church
Tell it to the man on death row
Tell it to the starving poor
Tell it to the sick and lame

Tell it to the rich folks
Tell it to the politicians
Tell it to the serial killers
Tell it to Wall Street

Tell it to the man on the gallows
Tell it to the chiseled faces
On Mount Rushmore
-
Tell it to the street whore
Tell it to the crack head
Tell it to the last wino on the Bowery

Tell it to the banker
Tell it to the butcher
Tell it to the unemployed

Tell it to the circus clown
Tell it to the insane
Tell it to the outlaw
Tell it to the panhandler
Tell me to the con man

Tell it to the baby found stuffed
In a dumpster
Tell it to the displaced factory worker

Tell it to the elderly
Tell it to the last alien hiding out in Roswell
Tell it to the militia

Tell it to the FBI sharpshooters at Ruby Ridge
Tell it to the arsonists at Waco Texas
Tell it the Indians at Standing Rock
Tell it to the junkie with dry heaves

Tell it to the farm worker
Tell it to the dishwasher
Tell it to the orderlies
Tell it to the flag waver

Tell it to the Chinese peasant toiling
In the rice fields for a dollar a day

Tell it to the garment worker
Slaving away in sweat shops
In Chinatown and the Latin Quarter

Tell it to the garbage man
Tell it to big business
Tell it to Corporate America
Tell it to the Supreme Court
Tell it to the blood stained NRA

Tell it to the Fascist President
Tell it to the oil barons
Tell it to the tobacco merchants

Tell it to the fur industry
Who club baby seals to death
For the clothing merchants
Tell it to the Priests Tell it to the Vatican
Tell it to the battered wives of America

Tell it to the pharmacy industry
Profiting off the sick and lame
Tell it to the millions of people
Dying from air pollution
In Mexico China and India

Tell it to the man on his deathbed
Not sure why he lived
Or what he is dying for

Tell it to Jesus Christ
Shout it to the stars
Line the traitors up against the wall
Rewrite the Ten Commandments
And start all over again

FROM MY WINDOW

I watch him shadow boxing
In his living room
His curtain open to the world
Free admission
No questions asked

A giant Doberman
Ears pinned back in attack mode watches pants
As the old man bobs and weaves
Shadow-boxing an imaginary opponent

From my vantage point across the way
I watch him jab a left hook an uppercut
Duck bob and weave
No trainer no corner man
To throw in the towel

I imagine him in the ring bleeding
Out of breath knocked down
Taking the mandatory eight count

Getting back up again
Beating the ten count
Knows like the rest of us
He can't win can't beat the odds
But refuses to throw in the towel

Nose bleeding head pounding
Jabbing punching going the distance
Hoping to get something better than a draw

POEM FOR GINSBERG

"I saw the best minds of my generation"
Destroyed by success and greed
Smug fashionable poets turned businessmen
Who rode the National Endowment For the Arts pimp train
Ignoring Captain Cool and his magic airplane

"I saw the best minds of my generation"
Loitering at closed down amusement parks
Disguised as hobo tramps
Standing in long lines in hope of becoming
A Southern Pacific Railway detective

Self-proclaimed geniuses tossing restlessly in their sleep
Like a pair of naked dice on a worn Las Vegas craps table
Their ragged claws scraping at death's window ledge

"I saw the best minds of my generation"
Lying lifeless in glass coffins
Hands folded in gratification
Their vacant eyes blinking like a pinball machine

"I saw the best minds of my generation"
Hanging out at Broadway topless bars
Searching for paradise fat and content
Smoking Tijuana slims
Stone-faced magicians on their way to the graveyard
Three steps behind the screaming organ grinder
With the one-eyes monkey masturbating on his back

"I saw the best minds of my generation"
Looking like James Bond understudies
Cruising the casinos of Reno and Las Vegas
In between being chauffeured through
The neon lit streets of Atlantic City
Looking for the Now Wow vision of their
Personal Zen masters

Pretty-faced aging celebrities
Hungry for the admiration connection
Who carried the star-fuck media message
Inside their chemically induced minds
Who wealthy and overcome with ego
Wandered the streets butter-cheeked
And Crisco greased in search
Of their 15 minutes of fame

"I saw the best minds of my generation"
Walking down Hollywood and Vine
Tossing and turning in exclusive spas
Ignoring the long lines of hungry eyes
Waiting to devour them
Who floated across heavily congested LA freeways
Looking for the right off-ramp
Stopping to partake the pleasure of heated
Swimming pools and Roman orgy bath houses
All the time contemplating their navels
And recording contracts

"I saw the best minds of my generation"
Bare their not so tight assholes
To aging agents wrapped in silk sheets
Autographed by the King of the Beats

"I saw the best minds of my generation"
Gang-banging ageless groupies
From San Francisco to New York and back
While accumulating frequent flier miles
Sad-eyed space cadets from the
Gregory Corso School of bad boys.

"I saw the best minds of my generation"
Expelled from luxury hotels for writing
Bad graffiti in the men's room
Who necked in the back alley of Gino and Carlo's Bar
While hawking their poetry in between ATM withdrawals

"I saw the best minds of my generation" cowering
In New York subways on their way to literary parties
Lusting after host and hostess alike

"I saw the best minds of my generation"
Standing naked in fear
Burning out there counterfeit talent
At Sardi's and Elaine's
As the final hours came closing in on them

"I saw the best minds of my generation"
Listen in terror as the 4-walls came crashing
Down on them
Lady obscurity coming to claim them
Like a faceless hatcheck girl
Let loose in the morgue's of America

THE LAST RODEO

strange this trip back in time
not with flesh and blood but
in the disguise of poems
having survived all these decades
the muscles the cells all changing dying
yet somehow managing to survive

I travel through a time tunnel through
an origin you cannot remember because
there is no you to remember it

I walk behind my shadow
shed the years like a snake sheds its skin
I who have never called myself a poet
never clothed myself in consonants and vowels
nor took refuge in similes or metaphors
yet plant the words on the page like
a florist preparing a bridal bouquet

a tender arrangement of flesh and bones
at war with the demons who leave behind
a Custer massacre of words
left cooking these images like
a skilled fry cook at a greasy diner

I wake at three in the morning
with junkie like sweats
my eyes a heat seeking missile
honed in on an invisible kill

left feeling like an alcoholic with the DT's
trying to roll a cigarette atop a bucking bull
at the world's last rodeo

EARLY MORNING TENDERLOIN POEM

Street cleaning truck rolls down the street
Like a tank on a mission
Hoses down the bag lady while across the street
Sweet Mary adjusts her hose
Tries to hide the track marks from
The undercover Narc's

She walks her beat looking for a white man
In search of a chocolate treat.

Street cleaning truck makes its second round
Washes down urine infested streets
Cleans up the city for the nine-to-five crowd

Hoses down the nightmares masking
The American dream
Reality a glass of warm beer
And a shot of Jim Beam

THINKING BACK TO THE PAST

after my shift at the Post Office
I'd stop for a drink at the corner bar
and chat with Carl the German bartender
but mostly I'd just sit there
and listen to the jukebox

and there was this guy who came in every night
and punched, B-5, Ray Charles singing
BORN TO LOSE

and I'd order another drink
and watch the bar clock tick down
bone ass tired from sorting tons of letters
fingers numb from stuffing them into pigeon holes

and I smelled of sweat and death
and kept drinking until I felt good
or ran out of money or both
and rode the 14 Mission bus home
with other people like me
who stared ahead or out the window
or down at their feet

night people like me who couldn't do
a nine-to-five job
and when I got off the bus
I walked that long three blocks to my apartment
and poured myself a drink
and turned on the stereo

and plopped my tired ass down on the bed
and let Billie Holiday sing me to sleep

NEW YEARS DAY 2019

Certain things stick in your mind
Like dental cement
Your first kiss
The Kennedy assassination
The wild years
A trip down Highway 101
Foot stuck to the gas petal
Hugging the middle lane
At eighty miles an hour

The clock strikes midnight as I attack
The keyboard with vengeance
The hour hand gone mad

Cursed with insomnia
I take a 5 AM walk through
The streets of Noe Valley
The hour of reprieve when
The shops are closed
The people sleeping
My neighborhood a ghost town
Still as a lion waiting on its prey
2018 gone the revelry put to rest

I greet the new year alone
With words that bleed for company

Back home a poem forms
Nibbles at my brain cells

A beggar hungry for food
But the cupboard is empty

 I retreat into the amnesia of yesteryear
The lost treasure of my youth
A pirate with a graying beard
Destined to board over and over again
A midnight ghost ship rocking aimlessly at sea

MEMORIES

I slip back in time
I'm driving down Highway One where
California fertile hills wink at me

Giant trees and seashore merge as one
Cloud banks ride the horizon like
Red Cloud rode the plains
In search of the last buffalo

Sweet mango's and watermelon wine
Sweet as cotton candy
Stuck to the roots of my tongue
Fed my youth nourished my spirit
The poem the language in my soul

Your body indented against mine
Hot as an iron pressed to a garment

Youthful hunger that knew no bounds
Feasted like a condemned man
Devouring his last meal

The way Eskimos used to swallow
The tears of the dying
To keep the one gone with them

SUNDAY THOUGHTS

Some poets write with speed
As if trying to stay one step ahead of death
Some write with the precision of a tailor
Wanting each line to be a perfect fit

Some poets toy with poems
Use each word as a building block

Some write hoping for a literary reputation
Some with the hope of luring women to bed

Today a poet editor invited me
To submit a poem on the topic of fame

I'd ask him for money
But long ago gave away my soul for free
Being a poet
I'm already a millionaire

BAYSHORE JUNK YARD

What's left of a classic "54" Thunderbird
  Lays like a war zone corpse
  Left to die a slow death
Hubcaps gone seats gutted interior
Steering wheel pushed into dashboard
She waits on the auto crusher
To clutch her in its steel claws
To come down on her
Like a crazed serial killer
Mutilated raped ravished
All life squeezed out of her once virgin frame

IMMIGRANT POEM

They cross the border looking
For a piece of the Promised Land
Entering a land that once belonged
To their ancestors
These conquered souls of Mexico
Who toil in fields of abundance
Harvest fruit and vegetables
With stooped backs and blistered hands
At pay no white man would consider
In a land built by immigrants
It now calls its enemies

POEM FOR WILLIAM BURROUGHS

you played the game out like a Mafia Don
late for an appointment with the God Father
you lived with the tenacity of a gunslinger
seeking another notch on his gun
your cinematic midnight cowboy eyes
cutup poster boy hero images
walking the minds third eye

a Cyclops trudging his way through
drug induced mythologies
grinding away the days the months the years
like a frenzied lap dancer seeking thrills
in forbidden pleasure zones

JAZZ ANGEL

she sits alone in her small hotel room
above the "222 Club"
in the heart of the Tenderloin
six months pregnant forced to give head
for soup and bread

no heat one wash clothe
one yellow stained washbasin
all hope bled dry

immigrant without visa or status
an illegal caught in a legal trap

feels the baby stir move inside her
heads for the door hears the
night manager whisper "whore"
suspended in silence and grief
floats face down in the bowels
of the American dream

WASTE LAND OF BLURRED VISIONS

I know this poet who plays
The Poetry Biz game
Knows how to trade favors
In 24 different flavors
His days pass faster than the
Muteness of his message

Seriousness is being treated like a sickness
A cancer to be avoided
Its grand slams and elite poetry festivals
Run by Grand Marshals and their elves

The wasteland of blurred visions
Lies like an idle landmine waiting
To explode in the minds of circus clowns

My poet friend has money in the stock market
Money in the bank
Money under his mattress

He's like a stand-up comedian
A burlesque dancer with see-through fans

To him a crisis is a loose bowel movement
A skipped heartbeat or two
But what of the crisis of the social system
A system of calculated murder
A system of chemical and environmental cancer
A system of the poor and elderly
A system of sadness

How do I laugh about this
How do I laugh about my brothers in prison
My dead comrades racing across blood stained clouds
Their bruised feet bringing down rain
A rain that does not cleanse but
Leaves behind scars and torn flesh

And still the games go on
Red poets who write love songs for Stalin
Populist poets turned businessmen
Hanging out at coffee houses
And uptown bars
Hoping for a lottery chance at fame
I can't wear the easy grin
It is an ill-fitting suit
My mind is a tailor who fits me
With needled threads

And yes there is a place for laughter
And I too can pen a funny line
But poetry is more than laughter
More than stepping up on stage
One hand on the poem
The other on the applause meter

It was a Russian poet who said
"The function of poetry must be
To make us blush with shame."
And it was an American poet who said
"The dams reverse themselves and want
To go stand alone in the desert"

That is why these poems are sad
The long-dead running over the fields

The masses sinking down
The light in the children's faces
Fading at six and seven

These are the voices I heed
Knowing the poet must believe
In what he says and writes
That a poet's responsibility
Goes beyond the written word

A poet must be angry
But he must be able to sing too
His words must melt like sweet honey
On a blistered tongue

For flat-backed whales sing and birds sing
But my poet friend has forgotten how to sing
It shows in his eyes
It shows in his nervous laughter

My poet friend writes 365 poems a year
He spends his time in coffee houses courting
The favors of those in power
He does not visit the jails
The prisons the forests the urban slums
The freezing North Dakota dawn
He does not feel the whisper
Of the secret that passes over the plains

DANCING WITH WORDS

There are poets who like
To dance with words
But dancing for an audience isn't like
Moving to the music on your own

Fame kills:
Billie Holidays ghost attests to this

Power corrupts
The scriptures tell us this
The true poet knows this
Stands tall above the
Dancing with word poets
Who are little more than
Instruments of a poem greater
Than themselves

Be like Li Po and sail your poems
On streams and puddles written on leaves
Be like the anonymous poets of Poland
During the height of martial law
Dropping their poems into the public square
For the people to read
Giving them courage and hope

Risk your life. Your literary life
For the people who need something
To cling to in desperate times

Telling the people how cruel their tormentors are
Won't inspire them to go on living
And overcome oppression

Love them become one with them
Stand fearless in their midst
This is the mark of the true poet

Walt Whitman was the John Lennon of poetry
Stood tall and fearless against the enemy
That is never really man but the
Poison in his soul, pride envy and lust

How can those afflicted with the disease of egomania
Jealousy and desire for fame and fortune
Write about and from the heart?

One column of media praise is of less value
Than a single teardrop on a poem
From a waitress in a greasy spoon diner

These people know nothing of genius
How can cockroaches evaluate eagles?
The true poets topic is people
Not the poet

SIX AM POEM

laying here alone in bed
a gnawing hunger in my belly
waiting to take my aching bones
to the kitchen table
take my morning does of pills
sad there is no woman to put them next
to my morning cereal

GRAND SLAM NIGHT

the lights are low
you can see the sweat beads bathe his face
like a lizard's tongue

the crowd is standing on its feet
screaming dancing whistling
stomping their feet to the tune
of a marching band

he's gyrating his hips
he's making love to the mike

his words are thunder
lightning bolts appear from nowhere
the poems are burning in his hands
the crowd is screaming for more

he's running up and down the aisle
reciting the ten commandments backwards

he's back on stage doing acrobatics
the audience is spellbound
the judges are frantically writing
down their scores

he's standing on his head
he's trying to raise the dead
he's brought in the Pope for a duet
the guy waiting his turn
looks white as a ghost

BETRAYED

As a child I thrilled
To the railroad trains
Riding out of the badlands
Not knowing they were owned
By robber barons

I watched the Calvary charge the
Indian villages like Attila the Hun
Believed Custer a hero and
Sitting Bull a savage

Not taught in school about the
Deadly smallpox plague
Diseased blankets traded Indians
For title to their land
A secret plot to murder
An entire nation

Generations of ripped-off cultures
Gather in the museum of history
Dolphins die in tuna fishermen nets
While pelican eggs refuse to hatch
Victim of man's greed and waste

The blistered hands
Of faceless migrant workers
Reach out for recognition
Only to find death in pesticide laden food

The tools of revolution laid aside
Rusting from affluence and false security

The dreams of hundreds of thousands
Of brave warriors lay buried
In unmarked graves
No historical monument
Will make mention of them

Their children buried in graves so small
Their parents wear them in their hearts
Like an anchor weighed
To the tip of their tongue

THE SYSTEM

There are old men and women
Who have worked all their life
Who have put in three four decades
For the right to a pension

There are old people who have
Worked twenty years or more
Only to be laid off and given
A two weeks severance check
To seek a living at half the pay

There are old people
Who have given their lifeblood
Only to witness the company go belly-up
And find there is no pension fund left

You can find them on park benches
Or wandering sterile supermarkets
Or sitting at neighborhood bars
Nursing drinks like a blood transfusion

They come in assorted flavors
Like "Life Savers"

Some thin and balding
Some fat and sweating
Some complaining bitterly
Some too proud to let the pain show

Trapped by a belief in a system
That has abandoned them

For the most part they suffer in silence
Duly unnoticed
To be carted off in meat wagons
To be cut open by a coroner
Who sees them as morning cereal

Who goes about his business
 like a butcher thinking of dinner
Thinking of a glass of wine
Thinking of how it used to be
How it might have been
How it should have been

It's the way of life
It's the way of politicians and mice
It's the system where just trying to stay alive
Becomes a small victory

CHARLES BUKOWSKI

(God's Don't Cry)

He was a leper
An angel a barbarian
He had shark's teeth that drew blood
From friends and foes alike

He was a shot of whiskey
A fine Cuban cigar
A rattlesnake without a warning system

He was a shaman
A witch doctor
A racetrack tout
A long shot in a fixed race

He was a hit man
Who left behind a trail of blood
As his signature card

He was a geek
A bully a butterfly
A moth courting a light bulb

He was a hustler a con man
A defrocked priest who walked
The streets Of Los Angeles
Looking for absolution

He was a shyster a magician
A clown with the best act in town

He was the Pied Piper of Los Angeles
With a bevy of female vampires
Who followed him to hell

He was the King of San Pedro
A Hollywood cult hero
Who never understood
The meaning of zero
His boasted conquests
Put Don Juan to shame

He was the undisputed champion
Of the small press world
Ready to win at all costs
Be it by a KO or a low blow
And he cried in the shower
But God's don't cry
Or do they?

TAKING A TRIP BACK IN TIME

I drove the freeway to Tucson
1960's Hippie Era
pulled over twice by the police
long hair and California license plates
got me two citation warnings

three days in redneck country was like a year
drinking at Western bars with cowboys
who eyed me like an Indian escaped the reservation
unsure why I had come here
nothing beautiful nothing natural
except for the stunning evening sunset

a poet friend calls me says Ginsberg
has flown back from India
to become the resident Guru
of the love generation
as I rack up another warning ticket

cowboy drunks give new definition
to the word redneck
no room for compassion here
no room for poets
words like a campfire with no match
to light them die in the heat

I stop in the desert
pop open a bottle of water
have a one-way conversation with

a cactus plant, wonder what
my shrink would think

the beauty of solitude
I could have a million conversations
in a single morning dialogue

I return home keep a notebook
on my nightstand
write down my dreams
but when I wake in the morning
someone else handwriting is on the page

no one will identify the blood between the lines
see the ghosts walk the halls
hear their moaning songs

their presence a hungry vampire
devour my memory bank like
a starving wolf in the dead of winter
looking to fill his hunger on wild game
or words that cling to flesh like
a leech to a raw wound

SAN FRANCISO 2016

Gentrification run amok
Greedy silicon "tech millionaires
Sweep down on the City like
Vultures hungry for road kill

The homeless treated like criminals
Home prices averaging a million dollars
Evictions served up like candy on Halloween
Yuppies dining on blueberry scones
Big brother watching in over head drones

A Mayor who is a joke
A bus system that doesn't work
Head cases set loose on the streets
Punk rockers with rainbow colored hair
Women with nose rings and pierced genitals
Ginseng for tired blood

My illusions are fighting
A duel with my delusions
The last time I picked up
An airport white courtesy phone
The voice on the other end was mine

The dates on my calendar are blank
My answering machine speaks in Chinese
There's no prize in my crackerjack box

My hand holds my cock in contempt
My love life is an unread resume
With one too many references

I had a dream I was a gunrunner
Trading hardware for software
I want my picture on a cereal box
Not the back of a milk carton

The IRS is a legal shake down
The Pentagon a slaughterhouse

Jack the Ripper sliced and diced
His way through life
And he wasn't even a chef

Freud was impotent
But knew how to put on a show
Monks know the answer to life
But won't share it

You know you're in trouble when your shrink
Sells you his fantasies
Sends you a bill for his reality

My life has become a distraction
No additions no subtractions
When it becomes an abstraction
I'll know I've found success

The Old Italians Of Aquatic Park

the old men of Aquatic Park
are dying or dead
they spend their time playing Bocce Ball
lady death striking them down like bowling pins

the old men of Aquatic Park
are steeped in tradition
dark skinned dressed in sport shirts
and baggy slacks looking like bit actors
out of a 1950 movie
dancing the last waltz on the deck of the Titanic

the old men of Aquatic Park
sit on hard wood benches late in the day
their eyes taking in young women
moving left and right
as if at a tennis match
pausing to feed the pigeons using
their hands as cutting knives
to separate the crust from the bread
which they toss into the air like
rice at an Italian wedding
rise to brush the crumbs from their pants
one with a suit vest and tie
pulls at the gold chain holding his pocket watch
securely next to his heart

the old men of Aquatic Park
have the smell of garlic and pasta

embedded in their skin
Italy breathing in their heart

the old men of Aquatic Park
are dying off with grace and dignity
and a love for the old-world ways

there is something sad about being Americanized
there is something sad about growing old

the Bocce Ball rolls slowly along the grass
comes to rest like a hearse parked at an open grave

funerals await them
flowers scattered like empty promises

the mourners fewer in number
their ranks depleted
file slowly into their cars
disappear into the shadows
Of late afternoon monotony

Boccie Ball will resume in the morning
there are pigeons to be fed
wine to drink stories to tell
the thirst for life masked in the face of death

A CALL TO POETS

poets unite
forget about a career in poetry
and concentrate on the poem
quit turning out factory
assembly line poems
quit trying to imitate Bukowski

poets unite
listen to your brothers and sisters
quit being the first poet to read
and the first to leave
quit using words as a preaching tool
when all over the world people are dying
victims of murder and genocide
as we stand on stage
well fed begging for applause
playing to the audience
telling our most intimate secrets
pretending to be knowledgeable
when we know so little

rams out fucking sheep
poets playing trick-or-treat
politicians beating their meat
whores making it under the sheets
predators lined up with elbow grease
landlords waiting to cancel your lease

It's gotten so bad that you can't tell
the real from the elite
everyone wants to become
a carbon copy of themselves

take a number step up on stage
rattle the cage let loose your rage
be sure to have your cell phone on
the call you miss may be from God
as we rival Ringling Brothers
standing tall standing proud
working the crowd

I call for all poets
to put down their pens
six months of the year
spend the saved postage helping the homeless
I'll be the first to take the pledge

poets take a vow of silence
serve a holiday meal at Saint Anthony's
sell your signed copies of Bukowski
and give the proceeds to war victims
in Iraq and Syria

pay homage at Malcolm X's grave
ride a boxcar for Woody Guthrie
say 12 Hail Mary's for Ali
sing a song for Selena
say a prayer for Allen
take the Eskimo out of Eskimo Pie
rename Hooters bar "testicles"

and hire male waiters to serve
in jockey shorts

legalize prostitution
campaign to have cops arrested
for disturbing the "peace"
tell the pope that you're giving up drugs
and the church
to worship at the altar of Walt Whitman

make Patchen required reading
adopt a rescue dog
give up center stage ego driven mania
for a trip to the park at dusk
invest in yourself instead of interest
bearing bank accounts

meditate instead of masturbate
make love instead of fucking
drop a bomb on Naropa
to prove you're more than a poet junkie

take a bookstore owner to dinner
talk child talk translate gibberish
put ego aside put power aside
quit visiting Kerouac and Bukowski's graves

return to the real world
put the poet back in poetry
make me want to believe
in you again